Black's Picture Sports

FLY FISHING

Black's Picture Sports

FLY FISHING

Sports Illustrated · Revised by

John Veniard

Adam and Charles Black · London

This edition first published 1976 by A & C Black Ltd
35 Bedford Row, London WC1R 4JH

ISBN 0 7136 1610 5

Cover and all photographs: John Marchington

Authorised British edition
© 1976 A & C Black Ltd
Originally published by J B Lippincott Company in the
United States of America as *Sports Illustrated Fly Fishing*
by Vernon S Hidy and the Editors of Sports Illustrated
©1972 Times Inc (revised)

Set and printed in Great Britain by
Page Bros (Norwich) Ltd, Norwich

Contents

1 Introduction

Fly fishing is quite different from coarse fishing. Although you *may* stay in one spot for some time it is much more likely that you will find yourself roving the banks, stalking the fish, taking advantage of any cover, even crawling to a good casting position.

Game fish are, generally speaking, rather more selective in their feeding habits and it is necessary to know a good deal about insect life. You can then identify whatever creatures the fish are feeding on when you are at the bank, and produce from your tackle box something which is sufficiently like that insect to fool the fish.

When you have hooked him, the fish (usually trout) is a game fighter and will give you a fight before either surrendering to the net or (all to often) breaking free. Here again is another difference – the tackle you will use is generally lighter than that used in coarse fishing and much depends on the skill with which you play the fish. Here perhaps is the essence of the sport – that it is your skill against the trout's cunning. Fishing would be dull if the angler always won.

A fine stillwater Brown Trout

8

2 The Art of Fly Fishing

The aim of the fly fisherman is to deceive fish, by offering imitations of their natural food in a manner that copies the behaviour of the nymphs, hatching nymphs, floating flies, drowned flies and darting minnows which fish eat.

Basically, a nymph is the larva of an aquatic insect such as the caddis fly, mosquito or dragonfly. In fly fishing, it is more accurately the final stage when the insect is fully developed within the larvae skin, and just before it leaves the stream bottom to float to the surface. The wings unfold when the insect leaves the water for the air.

A hatching nymph is any insect in the act of hatching in the water. This dramatic stage of their life cycle brings them swimming up to the surface, where they take wing as flies immediately, or float momentarily in or on the surface film to dry their wings.

Floating flies imitated by the fly fisherman consist of any aquatic or land-bred insects which usually live by a particular stream, river or lake. Drowned flies are any of these insects struggling or inert beneath the surface.

Streamers and bucktail flies are used to imitate the minnows and other small fry eaten by fish.

A fly fisherman's success depends to a great extent upon his knowledge of the insects most common on or in the water at the time he is fishing his artificial flies. Some anglers use 'attractor' flies – which are not designed to look like any particular insect – such as the Royal Coachman, or Wickham's Fancy; but the 'deceivers', or copies of real flies, such as the Blue Dun, Crane Fly or

March Brown are far more effective when the trout are choosy, as they often are, in their feeding.

The sport of fly fishing is, then, concerned with the size, form, colour and behaviour of the trout's food in or on the water. The best fly fishermen are, therefore, amateur experts on insects who also understand the characteristics and behaviour of trout. With some practice and experience, you will be able to cast and manoeuvre the dry fly so it will bounce, skip, dance or float cleanly without drag. You will also be able to catch trout on the nymph fished deep in the water, and the more lively hatching nymph struggling up through the water in full view of the fish and, sometimes, the fisherman.

The novice fly fisherman can usually catch trout rather easily with streamers and bucktails ('attractors') such as the Grey Ghost, Mickey Finn and Muddler Minnow. Do not be misled, however, by early success in catching large fish on these lures. Streamer fishing is enjoyable, but most fly fisherman consider this of minor importance compared to the other techniques that have greater appeal to both the fish and fishermen.

The traditional wet fly, unlike the hatching nymph, is tied with a wing which imitates drowned insects of any kind drifting naturally with the current or struggling to regain the surface. Some fishermen tie one pattern of wet fly on the end of the leader, another pattern of wet (or dry) fly some 50 or 60 cm above, with yet another

Figure 1. The Brown Hackle is a deadly general-purpose fly whose body possesses the bronzed effect of beetles and whose hackles will 'swim' in the currents like the legs of a struggling insect

fly above that. These additional flies are called droppers. By casting across the stream, you can manoeuvre the flies into pockets and cross-currents as your cast swings downstream, catching individual trout on either fly. Many experienced anglers frown upon the use of dropper flies, but you should know about them and explore their possibilities during the early stages of your fishing career.

Starting young

3 Learning to Cast

As in most forms of angling, the first essential of fly fishing is competent casting. Although obvious to anyone who has done any sort of fresh-water casting, it is worth stating here that accuracy rather than distance is the initial goal. Distance will come in time. Meanwhile the novice who masters accurate casts of 10·5 m will take fish on almost any stream.

When you first attempt the basic overhead cast (pages 18–24), you will go through the motions in a simple, mechanical way. Gradually your casts will become a graceful, rhythmic, fluid action performed subconsciously, much as a sports car driver changes gears by 'feel' rather than by the mechanics involved. To carry the analogy a step further, your choice of fly rod is as purposeful a decision as is a driver's choice of car: you rod commits you to a certain action and style.

BASIC EQUIPMENT

Rods A fly rod with a stiff action, which allows greater accuracy and more delicate presentation, is usually the choice of the dry-fly man. A softer-action rod, due to the smoothness and evenness of the action and the sensitivity inherent in it, is traditionally preferred by anglers fishing the delicate wet fly. If your aim is to become versatile with one rod that will be suitable for a variety of conditions, you will select a medium-action rod. With such a sensitive yet powerful all-purpose rod, you can cast a dry or a wet fly by merely changing the fly and the leader connecting it to the line. Medium-action rods from 2·00 to 2·75 m long are available in either split cane or glass fibre.

But the fishing site must also be considered. For small streams, where distance is secondary to accuracy, the shorter, lighter rod is preferable. On large streams and lakes, where distance is often necessary, the longer rod is better because of its greater power.

Reels   In the choice between manually operated and automatic reels, the simpler manual reel is perhaps preferable. The automatic reel retrieves line at the touch of a finger, and some anglers want this time-saving feature when fishing big water. Whichever you choose, your reel should not be so heavy that you notice its weight while casting, yet large enough to hold casting line and 28 m of backing line for playing large fish.

Lines and leaders   Although there is a detailed analysis of lines and leaders in Chapter 4 (pages 35–40), a brief discussion is nevertheless in order here. When you first try the overhead cast on a lawn, you should select a line that works well with your rod. Of the various types of lines used in fly fishing, double-tapered line is unquestionably the best for all-round effectiveness. Double-tapered line starts with a small diameter at one end, gradually increases thickness to a mid-section of larger diameter, then tapers off again at the other end. Only one tapered end and the level mid-section serve in a cast. When the casting end becomes worn, reverse the line and use the other end.

Double-tapered lines come in a variety of thicknesses and, in general, the thicker, heavier lines are easier to cast. But here, since the only critic that counts is the trout, a compromise is necessary. From the trout's point of view, a fine, light line is better. It touches and enters the water with a minimum of disturbance, is itself less noticeable in the water and casts less shadow on the

14

Beginner's bad luck

A hand retrieve of the fly line

bottom. All such disturbances may register on the trout's radar. The popular line calipering 1·14 mm in the mid-section and tapered to 0·64 mm at the ends is easy to cast, but some anglers prefer a lighter line tapering from 0·89 to 0·51 mm. The synthetic leaders today, of nylon or platyl, are tapered, the smallest diameter being the end section, or point, to which the fly is attached. Again, deferring to the sensitivity of the trout, many skilful anglers recommend a light leader, 2·4 or 2·7 m long, tapering from 0·33 to 0·15 mm at the farthermost end – the point.

Just because some master anglers lay down exacting requirements for equipment, you need not assume that either you or the equipment must be just perfect before you will take fish. It is reassuring to know that experts stress the importance of short, accurate casts (such as you will learn first), as the best way, by and large, to take fish. The angler should make as short a cast as the situation permits, not only to maintain accuracy but to enable the fly to touch the water before the leader and to minimise slack in the line. Some experts have maintained that the moment when a fly touches is the only moment at which a trout will take an artificial fly for a live one. There are other important moments. Later on we will cover the techniques evolved to create such moments. For the present, your first step is to take rod in hand and practise the cast.

THE GRIP

To achieve a proper grip for casting, hold your hand palm up and lay the rod handle across the second joints of your fingers. Close your hand and rotate your wrist until your hand is in the position shown in Figure 2. Press your thumb down on the handle. Be sure to keep your thumb on top; its position is essential in uniting your action and that of the rod. Notice that the rod is gripped so that the reel extends below your hand in a vertical plane.

17

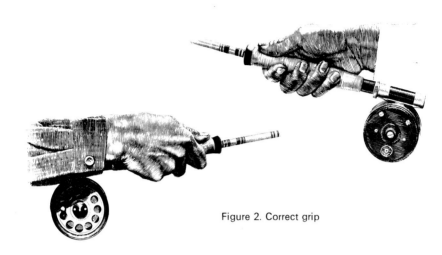

Figure 2. Correct grip

The position of your opposite hand (that is, the left hand of a right-handed caster) is also important; the angler constantly uses it to increase or decrease the amount of line in the air, and on or in the water. This hand is also used to retrieve line when manoeuvring a wet fly. As you start the overhead cast, the line should be hanging in a slack loop, held by the opposite hand at waist level, as shown in Figure 3.

THE OVERHEAD CAST

The overhead cast is the first one you learn, because it is the most often used method of presenting a fly. Moreover, it embodies the same basic principles as the sidearm cast and the forward part of the roll cast, which you will learn later. Many experts used to cast with the elbow pressed against the side, most of the power stemming from the wrist. The modern technique presented here, however, involving freer action of the whole arm, gives greater accuracy and is less tiring to the wrist.

Your arm, wrist and hand move much as they would if you were hammering a nail, with twist movement minimised to maintain control of the rod and preserve accuracy. When actually presenting a fly to the water, you perform the complete action shown in the following sequence (Figure 4A–E). To feed out more line or to dry a fly, you will often 'false-cast'. This involves following the action through 4A–D, but beginning a second backcast just before the fly touches the water. If you are lengthening line, in the forward part of each false cast you release some or all of the line you have been holding in your opposite hand.

To start, strip out 4·5 to 6 m of line through the rod guides and lay it out straight on a lawn. Then, gripping the rod and holding a slack loop of line with your opposite hand, as you have learned, face in the direction of the line running across the lawn. At the start of the cast you should be holding the fly rod in such a way that the tip is raised slightly above a line parallel to the ground.

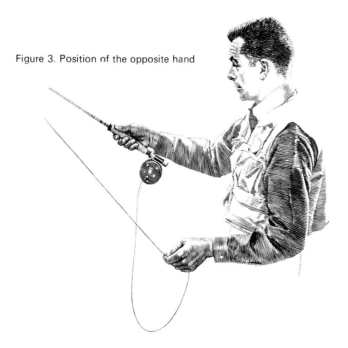

Figure 3. Position of the opposite hand

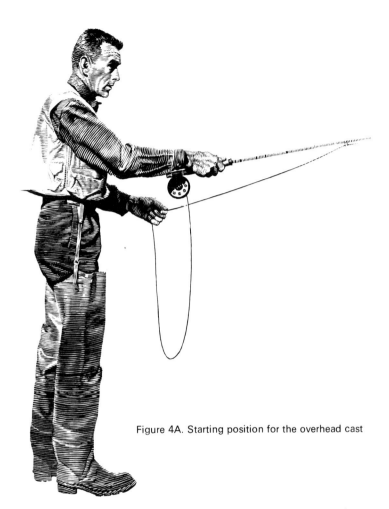

Figure 4A. Starting position for the overhead cast

Slowly raise the rod by lifting your upper arm and at the same time bending your elbow to bring your forearm towards your face. At this point, your opposite hand holds the line securely so that no slack line slips through the guides as you raise the rod. Illustrations 4B–E include diagrams of the lively, whiplike action of the rod and the flowing course your line will follow through the air when you learn to perform the actions reasonably well.

20

Figure 4B. Raising the rod

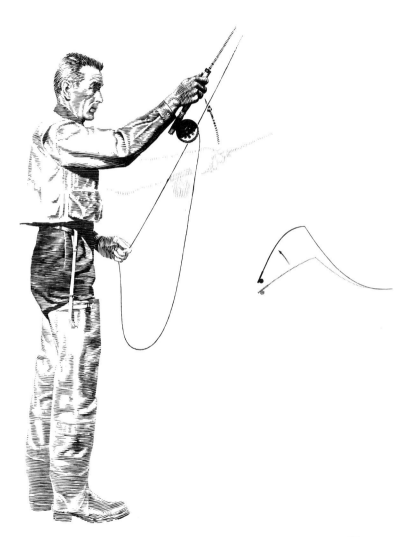

Figure 4C. Lifting the line off the ground

22

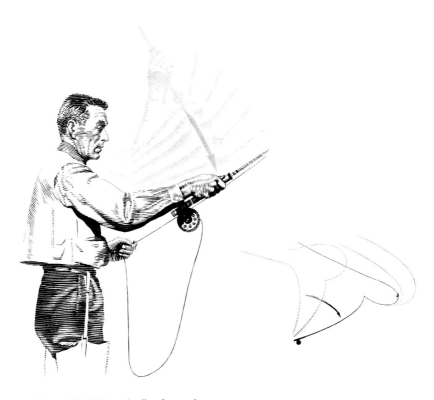

Figure 4D. Driving the line forwards

The third step in the overhead cast is to lift the line up off the ground. As you slowly raise the rod, when your forearm and rod are at an angle of about 45° to the ground (*shadow outline*), give a smart lift and then immediately stop when your forearm is nearly vertical. If you do this smoothly, the line will rise from the ground and move up and back. As the line continues backwards, relax your wrist somewhat so that the rod drifts backwards slightly. You will feel a tug as the line straightens out behind you.

The forward part of the cast begins as soon as the line straightens out behind. The instant this happens, slowly start to lower your upper arm while pushing forwards with your forearm. Through the flexion of the rod you will feel that you are pulling the line forwards. As the movement continues, the rod enters the power zone. When your arm and rod approach the 45° position, push hard with your thumb and wrist. This causes the upper part of the rod to drive the line forwards in a very tight loop.

As the line straightens out in front of you, release the slack line held by your other hand and the momentum will pull it forwards through the guides. As the line shoots through the guides, your rod should be back at the starting position. As the line falls, raise the rod tip slightly. This will not only put the fly down better, but the slight angle gives you a margin of safety: the flexion of the rod cushions the shock if a trout hits immediately. A fish with a direct pull on the line will very likely break the point.

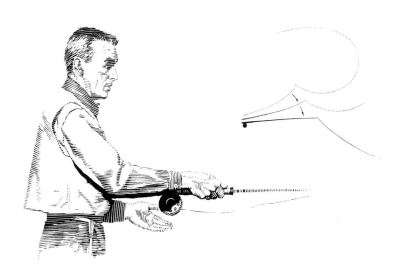

Figure 4E. The final position

Figure 5. The side-arm cast

THE SIDE-ARM CAST

Trees or high banks or other obstructions along a stream will often prevent you from performing the back part of an overhead cast. In such cases, where there is clearance to the side, you can cast side-arm so that the line travels over the water in a horizontal plane rather than vertically overhead. In side-casts you forfeit some accuracy and distance, but you can usually manoeuvre into a position that will allow you to present the fly in likely spots to take fish. In some cases, even when there is overhead clearance behind you, the side-arm is the only way of getting a fly under brushy overhang and other inaccessible places favoured by trout, and too often ignored by casual anglers. In steep ravines, too, when the wind is running strong, side-arm casts can help you by keeping the line low over the water.

The grip for the side-arm cast is similar to that for overhead casting, except that your rod and hand are rotated about 90°. Thus, the thumb is no longer on top but to the outside, lying in the plane of the horizontal sweeping action you are about to perform. As your hand is rotated to achieve this position, the reel now lies nearly horizontal. Discounting the slight effect gravity has on a line moving horizontally, the course of your line in the horizontal plane when you cast side-arm is identical to the course of the line in the vertical plane when you cast overhead. You can begin learning the side-arm cast on a lawn or on a stream. If you start on a stream you should first try it in an open area, where you can pay out some line first with overhead casts. Then, when you have the side-arm cast learned at least mechanically, you can try it in an obstructed area, where a great deal more finesse will be required.

At the start, you face the direction in which you intend to cast, with the casting arm extended but not straight or stiff. Your upper arm should be sloping down

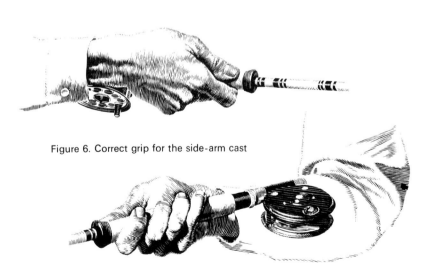

Figure 6. Correct grip for the side-arm cast

Figure 7 Close-up of the side-arm cast

at an angle of about 45°, your forearm and rod extended and slanting up a few degrees from horizontal. If you are a right-hander, your rod and forearm should be pointing a little to the right of the direction in which you intend to cast.

In the side-arm cast, as shown in Figure 8, swing your arm back until your forearm and rod reach a point roughly at right angles to the starting position. As you start this backward sweep, your wrist should be stiff so that forearm and rod move as a unit. But about midway in the sweep back, flex your wrist to the rear to power the line backwards. When the line straightens out behind

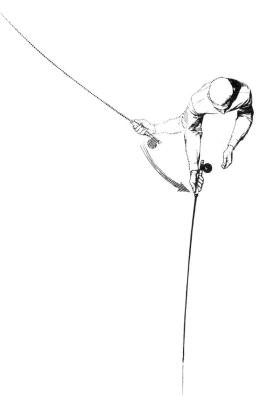

Figure 8. Overhead view of the side-arm cast

you – you will feel the tug on the rod – begin the forward cast, sweeping arm and rod back towards the starting position. In the first part of the return arc, the wrist remains flexed backwards. About midway, by straightening the wrist and pressing with your thumb, you shove the rod forwards. This action, as in the overhead cast, will cause the rod tip to flip the line in a tight loop towards the intended target.

THE ROLL CAST

The roll cast is particularly necessary when trees or other obstructions do not give you clearance for either overhead or side-arm casts. It can also be useful in placing a fly at a point directly upwind from the fisherman. Beyond these obvious values, there are others: there is a minimum of arm and rod movement to telegraph your presence to the fish, and in fishing a submerged fly the film of water on fly and leader is less disturbed by the roll cast, so that both sink more cleanly as they are put down on the surface. Also, when fishing deep, often you tempt fish by causing your fly to rise. You do this by raising your rod vertically, and from this position the most convenient cast is another roll cast. For other reasons equally important, which are covered in the discussion of stream strategy (see Chapter 6), the roll cast, although not so accurate as other casts, nor as good for distance, is a valuable part of your casting repertoire.

In the roll cast, as the name implies and the next sequence indicates, you draw the line towards you as you raise your rod. Then with a sudden motion of the arm you roll the line back out over the water. While you can start learning the overhead and side-arm casts on a lawn, you should start trying the roll cast on a stream or, better yet, on a still pond, where the smooth, even resistance of the water against the line helps achieve a satisfactory cast.

For the roll cast you take the same grip on the rod as for the overhead cast. Start with about 6 m of line on the water at your feet, preferably on the side of your casting arm. Keep 0·90 or 1·20 m of line slack between your other hand and the reel, as shown in Figure 9A. From this simple beginning you can make casts of up to 15 m, following the sequence of action explained here, using the other hand to strip out more line from the reel at the completion of each cast.

As you begin the roll cast, your wrist is held stiff, as in the overhead, so that forearm and rod are a single working unit. At the start of a cast, lift the rod by raising your upper arm and forearm as shown in 9B. You carry this motion through at a *slow* speed until the forearm and

Figure 9A. Starting position for the roll cast

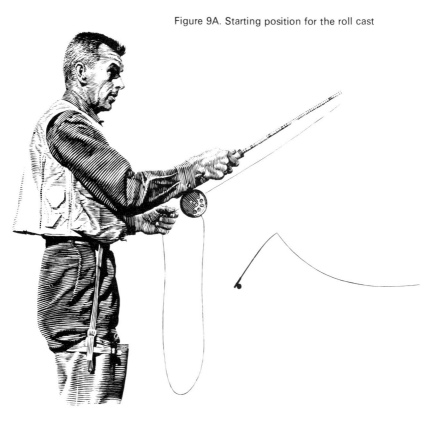

Figure 9B. Lifting the rod

Figure 9C. Final movements of rod and line

c

rod are overhead and actually inclining slightly to the rear. At this point you should make a definite pause so that the line, which has been pulled towards you through the water, now hangs slack near your side. Your wrist should remain slightly relaxed.

Forward movement of the cast is started by lowering your upper arm suddenly, while pushing forwards with your forearm. Give a thrust with your thumb as your arm moves forwards, as in the overhead cast, so that the rod tip will flip the line into a curling loop which will roll out over the water. The rod and line action for the start of the forward cast are shown in shadow. Final movements of rod and line are shown in 9C.

4 Lines, Leaders and Knots

If you care to, you can begin learning the side-arm cast on a stream or pond rather than a lawn. In any case, the third cast in your repertoire, the roll cast shown on pages 30–34, can best be learned on a stream. There you will need to know how to tie the knots joining line, leader and fly. Before you reach the water, here are some facts to guide you.

LINES

Of the types of line available, double-taper floating line is recommended as the best for general use. Single-taper line offers the same casting characteristics but has a shorter life, since the angler cannot reverse it when one end begins to wear. Level line, as the name implies, has no taper. Though cheaper, it is not recommended. The most that can be said for level line is that it will do in

LINES

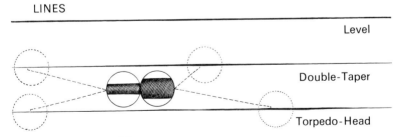

Level

Double-Taper

Torpedo-Head

Figure 10. Types of line

35

various situations, but is not really good in any. Another type, weight-forward or forward-taper line, has a thick, heavy section near the forward end which pulls the rest of the line through the guides more readily. Designed for distance, weight-forward line will cast accurately but with less finesse than the more delicate double-taper. The makeup of the various types of lines generally used in fly fishing is shown in Figure 10.

Unless your line is carefully matched to the particular characteristics of your fly rod, you will never be able to cast with full effectiveness. There are few decisions more important, with regard to equipment, than the purchase of line of the correct weight for your rod. Many rod manufacturers specify the appropriate line for each of their rods, but if you are not sure which weight to choose, consult a knowledgeable person in a tackle shop, bringing your rod with you. The AFTM's (Association of

STANDARDS

Designation Number	Weight in Grains* ($437\frac{1}{2}$ gr. =103)	Range (Manufacturers' tolerances)	FLYLINE SYMBOLS	FLYLINE TYPES
1	60	54— 66	L=Level	F=Floating
2	80	74— 86	DT=Double-	S=Sinking
3	100	94–106	taper	I=Intermediate
4	120	114–126	WF=Weight-	(Float or
5	140	134–146	forward	Sink)
6	160	152–168	ST=Single	
7	185	177–193	taper	
8	210	202–218		
9	240	230–250		
10	280	270–290		
11	330	318–342		
12	380	368–392		

* Weight is based upon the first 30 feet of line exclusive of taper or tip.
Example: DT-5-F is a double-taper line No. 5 floating line weighing 140 grains.

Figure 11. AFTM Flyline Standards, Symbols and Types

Fishing Tackle Manufacturers) recommended standards are shown in Figure 11. Floating line is preferred as the general-purpose fly line, and may be used for wet flies and nymphs on most streams and lakes. Sinking line is for special conditions when you need to fish a fly very deep. The dry fly is, of course, fished exclusively with the floating line. Many anglers – certainly for any extended fishing trip – have two or three sets of balanced rod and line combinations for various types of water.

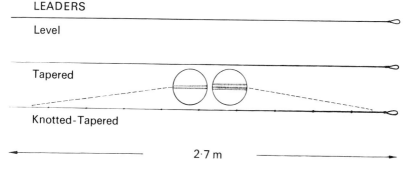

LEADERS

Level

Tapered

Knotted-Tapered

2·7 m

Figure 12. Types of leaders

LEADERS

An understanding of the characteristics of leaders is important in all fly fishing. The principal types of leader material used today are synthetics such as nylon, platyl and perlyl. Whatever the material, it is important that the leader does not glisten or glare in sunlight.

The flotation of synthetic leaders can be reduced by rubbing them with soap, mud, or the slime from a fish. To offset lightness some anglers tie up synthetic leaders with a forward taper or 'belly' of larger diameter towards the centre sections of the leader, offsetting the overall lightness of the leader by adding some weight at the point where it serves best to help carry the fly forwards.

37

To ensure against slipping, knots in the synthetics must be tied with extra care. Low temperatures may cause these materials to become brittle, and crack or break.

In general, heavier leaders serve well when fishing rough water, when using a large fly and when casting into or across a strong wind. Lighter leaders are essential in still, clear water, and when casting a small fly, and under bright, sunny conditions when even the slight shadow cast by the semi-translucent leader can be enough to scare the wary trout.

As with line, more delicacy of presentation is achieved with a tapered rather than with a level leader. The thicker end of a tapered leader is connected to the line; the small end is tied to the fly. Today, knotless, tapered synthetic leaders are the most popular, although some anglers prefer knotted leaders made up of 25 or 30 cm lengths of different thicknesses, tied in diminishing sequence to achieve a taper. Leader material varies in thickness and also in strength. Thicknesses are designated as 2x, 3x, 4x and so forth, with 'x' equalling 0·25 mm, 1x equalling 0·23 mm, 2x equalling 0·20 mm, and so on.

KNOTS

Of the variety of knots that anglers use, those illustrated in Figures 13–16 will do the whole job of combining all of the essential elements as you normally will use them.

Figure 13. Double loop

Double loop   With this loop tied in the end of the leader, you will need only a simple jam knot to connect leader to line. The loop should be about 13 mm in diameter.

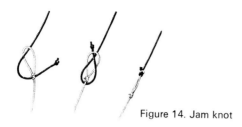

Figure 14. Jam knot

Jam knot Here is a simple, fast and reliable way of connecting the line to the double loop tied in the end of the leader.

Figure 15. Blood knot

Blood knot Used to join sections of level leader material of varying thicknesses in diminishing order for a tapered leader.

Figure 16. Turle knot

Turle knot Used to connect the leader point to the fly. In using gut, the knot is tied as it is shown here; but with platyl or nylon, in order to prevent any slipping, tuck the end back through the loop once more before drawing the knot tight, thus making a double-turle knot.

HOOKS

The quality of the hook is vital since the fly is only as good as the hook upon which it is tied. Soft hooks bend, brittle hooks break, so the temper of a hook is a prime consideration. You should test each box of hooks by bending one hook in a vice. To penetrate a trout's jaw, the point should be sharp; the barb, small. Hook styles and shapes are a matter of preference. Model Perfect and Sproat are very popular today. In Figure 17, hook sizes 10 to 20, shown for the Model Perfect style, are the sizes you will use most in imitating stream insects.

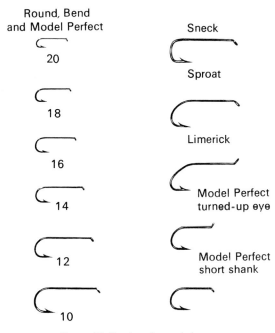

Figure 17. Hook styles and shapes

A typical loch trout

42

5 The Dry Fly

Fishing a floating fly is an extremely popular technique. The angler can always see the fly and the rise of a fish as he wades upstream exploring the water with casts. These are aimed somewhat above the water, so that the delicate fly may drop naturally and easily to the surface. Accuracy and finesse in presenting a dry fly to a large fish, which is feeding at intervals on floating insects, will test the nerve and skill of a novice. This is referred to as 'fishing the rise', in contrast to 'fishing the water' during those lulls or periods of inactivity when no fish are seen feeding at the surface.

Before the dry fly is allowed to drop to the water, the angler makes several false casts to dry the fly. False casts also pose and answer two vital questions: is there ample clearance of weeds, bushes or trees for your backcast? and – equally important – is the amount of line coiled in your left hand and moving in the air adequate for reaching the exact piece of water you have chosen to place your fly? With or without a wind blowing against, across or with the direction of your cast, false casts are essential preliminary tactics for the angler fishing upstream, downstream or across the stream.

Just as sudden changes in the direction or velocity of the wind may force the dry-fly angler to pause or stop fishing momentarily, the appearance of a large trout feeding in another section of a pool or a riffle may suggest a minor or major change in strategy. Catch the smaller trout feeding recklessly if you must. Move promptly, however, into position for deceiving the larger fish which will be more selective and more challenging. This may involve cutting back your leader from 0·45 kg to the 0·91 kg section a length of 20 or 25 cm as a rule. It may involve changing to a fresh new fly, and it can often indicate a change in your position in the river for the most advantageous presentation of your fly to this desirable fish.

A methodical, deliberate approach to fishing the dry fly can be productive, of course, but versatility and awareness of changing or new opportunities are always the hallmarks of an imaginative, experienced fly fisherman. The changes involve, for example, the appearance of one or more insects during the course of an afternoon or evening; sudden variations in the weather; constant new problems encountered in moving along pools, around rocks, obstacles or bridges; and incidental information you pick up from other fishermen or by examining the stomachs of trout. These and other factors can have a direct bearing on the many decisions and choices open to a dry-fly fisherman moving up or down a stream.

USING THE WIND

The dry fly activated by the wind is often irresistable to trout. Even in ordinarily tranquil pools the surface is broken enough to lower the chances of a fish seeing you or your leader. You are able, therefore, to move in and fish with a shorter line, often from the bank near a good spot. With a short length of line and the leader extending from the rod, let the wind skim and bounce the dry fly on and off the water. In certain circumstances, a longer line can be used with the rod held high and moved to shift your fly from one feeding lane to another, or along the edges of floating or sunken logs.

CASTING UPSTREAM

Ideally, you should present your fly above and to the

A nice fish nearly ready for the net

side of a feeding fish, so that it does not see either your leader or your line. Always let your fly float one or two metres downstream from the fish before lifting the fly from the water. The fish may be following it, as they often do in fast water, and be about to take it. Also, there may be another fish below ready to take a lively floating insect moving naturally with the current. The rule, then, is to fish out every cast until the fly begins to drag or move unnaturally.

The retrieval of your dry fly should be made slowly to avoid disturbing the water or wetting the fly unnecessarily.

Retrieving line Assuming you are standing in the water and have cast upstream at a slight angle, reach up and take the line between your thumb and forefinger just below the first line guide on your fly rod. Depending on the speed of the fly floating towards you, pull the line through the guides to remove or avoid any slack line between the end of your rod and the fly. As the line is pulled in, catch it beneath the forefinger of your hand holding the fly rod. This ensures a minimum of slack line between your rod tip and any fish rising to your fly. Although a certain number of fish may virtually hook themselves, far more will eject the fly unless the angler reacts instantly by raising the rod tip to set the hook. For this reason slack line must be avoided and controlled.

Some anglers prefer to coil the retrieved line in loops in their left hand while others let the line float downstream behind them. Careful handling of retrieved line, in any event, has other advantages that cannot be ignored by any angler: you are always prepared for perfect shooting of the line on your next cast, and your line will flow smoothly through the guides during the first powerful run of any big fish.

CASTING DOWNSTREAM

In various situations, especially above natural obstacles,

a dry fly must be floated downstream from the angler to the fish. Here, an important advantage for the angler is that the fish will see the fly before it sees the leader, since it is facing upstream. However, rather than retrieve line, the angler must carefully release it to avoid excessive slack line at the instant of a strike.

One tactic useful in open water is rather a high cast above a feeding fish, and a sharp pull on the rod which brings the fly back upstream and allows the line to fall to the water in a series of S-shaped loops. Depending on the current or cross-currents, you may mend your line or release more line as required to float the fly into the feeding zone of the fish.

The downstream float beneath overhanging bushes or branches is often very effective, because such places offer fine protection for trout as well as a constant supply of food. Both aquatic and terrestrial insect imitations can be used since grasshoppers, beetles and ants frequently fall to the water here, and fish often rise to sip these into their mouths, causing only a small dimple on the water. Unless the angler is alert for this almost imperceptible rise, he will miss the fish. Or, should the fish hook itself, the prize can be easily and instantly lost in the bushes or the roots beneath the water. In setting the hook in such fish, the angler should keep his rod tip near the water to avoid jerking the fly up into the branches when the fish misses the fly or strikes short.

One of the most exciting and dramatic moments in fly fishing is the initial float of a dry fly to a large trout feeding at the upper edge of reeds or an underwater obstacle. Like many large fish, they often rise at rather predictable intervals, ranging from 10 to 20 seconds when flies are plentiful during a hatch. This suggests, as a rule, that your fly should arrive some few seconds after the fish has taken a fly. Also, if the fish is over 1·4 or 1·8 kg, you must be prepared to exert strong pressure immediately to keep the fish from the obstacles. Once the fish is out in the open currents, hold your rod high and let him run against the line on your reel, retrieving line at intervals between runs without undue pressure at any time unless he goes towards the obstacle.

Retrieving line At the end of a downstream float of the dry fly, the retrieve of your fly must be made slowly to avoid disturbing the water. Before retrieving or during the retrieve, a hesitant fish may be tempted to strike by twitching the fly, especially in rather rough or broken water. In any event, steer the fly away from the more promising water during the retrieve. With a floating line you can lift line, leader and fly with a sharp back-cast after retrieving all but 6·0 or 7·5 m of line. Make several false casts to dry the fly and you are ready for another presentation.

It must always be borne in mind that many rivers have rules forbidding the use of the downstream cast, and these should be rigidly observed.

6 Choice of Flies

All dry flies represent winged insects, and most dry flies represent either the upwinged fly or the caddis fly. Also, most dry-fly patterns are direct imitations of natural insects – deceivers – rather than the brighter-coloured attractors. Both types of flies catch fish, but the more orthodox, conventional deceivers deserve the attention of the beginner far more than the attractors, which seem to appeal to fishermen more than to the fish, especially browns and rainbows.

Other important distinctions should be considered when selecting dry flies, according to the rivers or lakes you will fish and, to some extent, your personal prefer-ences for delicate, lifelike flies as well as durability, buoyancy or visibility. No single pattern possesses all four qualities, any one or two of which can be decisive in catching fish under certain conditions.

TYPES OF DRY FLIES

Figure 18.
Blue Dun

49

Divided wing flies These suggest the upwinged fly floating along shortly after its emergence from the water. Imitations should have stiff hackles, delicate tapered bodies, stiff tail fibres and natural proportions with balance in order to float properly. Some popular patterns are Blue Dun, March Brown and Ginger Quill.

Figure 19.
Sedge fly

Downwing flies These suggest caddis flies, sedges, stone flies and grasshoppers etc that have dropped to the water. Stiff hackle and wings that slope back above the rather prominent body are the important features of this fly. Some popular patterns are the Brown and Green Sedge, Large Brown Sedge, Silverhorns, Cinnamon Sedge, Great Red Sedge, Grouse Wing, Muddler Minnow, Murrough and Green Peter (Irish Patterns).

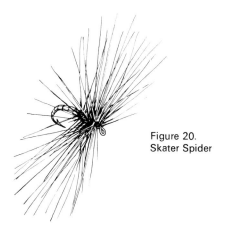

Figure 20.
Skater Spider

Spider and variant flies These suggest any insect, especially delicate insects, because they are tied on rather small hooks with relatively long, stiff hackles, which drop so lightly on the surface that a slight breeze can cause them to twitch or jump. Some popular patterns are Badger Variant, Ginger Spider, Multicolour Variant and Blue Dun Spider.

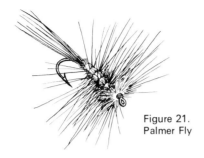

Figure 21.
Palmer Fly

Palmer flies   These also suggest many types of insects and offer both buoyancy and visibility. They are most effective in fast, rough or broken water with natural float, bouncing or skimming near the edges of the current. Some popular patterns are the Soldier Palmer, Red Palmer, Olive Palmer and Blue Dun Palmer. When tied with a white hackle in the front, they become what are known as 'Bi-visible' flies, a type very popular in the USA. The extra white hackle is for increased visibility.

Hairbodied flies   These are tied with bodies of clipped deer hair to represent any of the larger insects. Extremely buoyant in the roughest water, the bodies are very durable and the wings are usually quite visible. Some popular patterns are the Irresistible, Humpy and Rat-Faced McDougall.

Parachute flies   For these flies, hackles are tied parallel to the shank of the hook. All the hackle fibres therefore float, in or on the surface film, in a lifelike manner with good visibility and buoyancy. Popular patterns are Red Quill and Pale Watery.

Terrestrial flies   Used to imitate land insects such as beetles, ants, worms and crickets, that drop to the water. These flies are usually fragile and have poor visibility. Some popular patterns are the Black Ant, Red Ant and Coch-y-Bonddu Beetle.

Midge flies   These represent and suggest very small insects of any kind, some of which have a great appeal to the trout. They have poor visibility, limited durability but rather good buoyancy. Some popular patterns are the Black Gnat, Grey Midge and Cream Midge in sizes 20 and 22, which require 6x or 7x points, since the eyes of these hooks are very small.

STREAMERS BUCKTAILS AND LURES

Figure 22. Streamer design

When the water is high and discoloured, many species of freshwater and saltwater gamefish will take lures that imitate various minnows, parr, fry etc. As a knowledge of insects is useful in fly fishing, some knowledge of the small fish inhabiting the water you plan to fish will be helpful in selecting successful lures. As a rule, streamers and bucktails are cast above likely holding water, and retrieved within view of the fish with an erratic, twitching motion that simulates the behaviour of an injured minnow. Such a presentation may appeal to a fish's hunger, rapacity, playfulness or curiosity.

Most streamers and bucktails are brightly-coloured attractors with silver tinsel bodies and colour combinations of yellow, orange, red, brown or grey and the shape and form and size of baitfish. Deceiver patterns are more carefully designed to imitate specific small fish such as the fry of the rainbow, brown trout, salmon and other fish. Lifelike swimming action is achieved with long feathers in the streamers and long hair in the bucktails, although some patterns combine both feathers and hair in varying amounts. To facilitate hooking a fish, most streamers and bucktails are tied on long-shanked hooks and some are tied tandem on two hooks, that are connected by a piece of synthetic leader material. You are more likely to use this type of fly or lure on open stretches of water such as lakes and reservoirs, and there are many hundreds of patterns to choose from. Some of the best known are the Black Lure, Badger Lure, Church Fry, Polystickle, Muddlers, Jersey Herd, Sweeney Todd, Chief, Grey Ghost and Matuka.

Trout rising steadily

7 Nymph Fishing

By definition, all nymphs are larvae of aquatic insects and resemble, to some extent, the winged insects they will become after they mature. As nymphs they have no wings, of course, and burrow into the silt or vegetation and hide in the gravel or natural debris on or near the stream bed. According to their habitat and method of locomotion, nymphs have been divided into four categories: burrowers, swimmers, crawlers and clinging flat nymphs.

Trout feed on these nymphs at all stages of their development, methodically searching the stream bed' for nymphs or nymph cases on stones or aquatic plants. Artificial nymphs fished deep are often effective, therefore, early in the season when the water is high or discoloured from the spring runoffs. They are also effective later in the season when there is no insect activity on the surface of a stream or lake.

Nymphs should be fished to sink and move naturally with the currents. Cast upstream or diagonally up and across the stream, a fish may take the nymph at any time during the drift, but most fish are hooked as the nymph reaches the lower end of a drift and just prior to your retrieval. The swing with the current causes the nymph to rise in a manner that attracts the fish.

Nymph fishing in lakes often requires a fast-sinking or extra-fast-sinking line to get the lure down into the feeding zone of the fish. A rather slow retrieval with frequent pauses will cause the nymph to ascend and descend in a lifelike manner. At times the angler must experiment with various speeds of retrieval and at various depths in order to succeed. Once you discover a combination acceptable to the trout, you will do well, as a rule, if you repeat the presentation exactly as before. Such minor considerations are often decisive in nymph fishing.

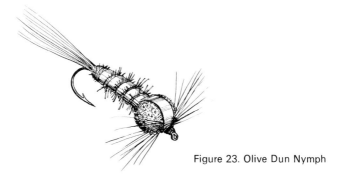

Figure 23. Olive Dun Nymph

Although nymph patterns have not been standardised as much as dry flies and wet flies, some of the more popular patterns today include the following: Blue Dun, Iron Blue, Olive Dun, Green Peter, May Fly, Pale Watery Dun, March Brown, Lake Olive Dun, Pheasant Tail and Greenwell.

8 Trout Stream Insects

Artful presentation of a fly is easier for the angler who understands the behaviour and identity of trout stream insects. The descriptions offered here give only the most obvious differences and similarities between insects. Trout eat with their eyes, so to speak, sensing and appreciating naturalness of both the fly and the behaviour of the fly. Therefore, the angler who can coax a fly to behave naturally must understand the aquatic peculiarities of various insects. He must know what fly to use and how to present it.

A lifetime champion of the wet fly, the late G E M Skues wrote: 'The indications which tell your dry-fly angler when to strike are clear and unmistakable, but those which bid a wet-fly man raise his rod point and draw in the steel are frequently so subtle, so evanescent and impalpable to the senses, that when the bending rod assures him that he had divined aright, he feels an ecstasy as though he had performed a miracle each time'.

The insects most often eaten by trout come under the following orders:

Upwing flies, including mayflies . . . *Ephemeroptera*
Caddis fly . . . *Trichoptera*
Stone fly . . . *Plecoptera*
Mosquitoes, gnats, midges, crane fly . . . *Diptera*
Ants, bees . . . *Hymenoptera*
Grasshoppers . . . *Orthoptera*
Dragonfly, damsel fly . . . *Odonata*
Alder fly . . . *Megaloptera*
Beetles . . . *Coleoptera*

Figure 24. May fly

UPWINGED FLIES

The upwinged fly deserves first mention because of its universal appeal to trout. Lively swimmers, the nymphs are all aquatic. Most species swim upwards through the water to hatch, tantalising trout and offering the angler a fine chance to match the struggling nymph with a copy in size, form, colour and hackle-leg action.

Stage two, the subimago on the surface, calls for a dry fly, as does stage three, the imago or spinner stage of mating and egg-laying. The Ginger Quill, March Brown and Blue Dun are deservedly famous fly patterns, tied with upright wings characteristic of these two stages and designed to float.

Stage four, the spent spinner, brings the wet fly into play for imitating the struggling, drowning insect.

Any species of upwinged fly may hatch at intervals over a period of several days. Tuesday's hatching nymph for example, may be Thursday's spent spinner in the water simultaneously with Thursday's batch of hatching nymphs. Some noted anglers have fished many upwinged fly imitations on the theory that a wet fly could represent either the ascending nymph of stage one or the drowning fly of stage four. Such patterns are tied without a wing and a soft or medium hackle, usually a Blue Dun or Honey Dun.

Figure 25. Caddis fly

CADDIS FLY

So beloved by trout, caddis flies are often eaten case and all. Caddis larva may be seen on the bed of almost any stream or lake. As the larva matures, it enlarges its camouflaged home until it reaches the pupal stage. Then it seals off the entrance for about two weeks, finally emerging as an exciting swimmer in full view of the trout.

This significant similarity to the hatching upwing fly nymph makes the ascending insect movement simulated by the 'Lift' (see page 88) important to a wet fly angler, for all trout understand it. Also, the fact that the food is *escaping* somehow triggers otherwise hesitant trout into striking, often just beneath the surface with a deliberate, twisting satisfaction.

Figure 26. Caddis larva in case

The descending fly, also, is a useful wet-fly tactic, for the female of some caddis species crawls or swims down into the water to deposit her eggs after mating. The Hare's Ear, Dark or Light, for instance, is often taken soon after it touches the water since it has a natural counterpart in the female caddis impassioned by instinct to reach an underwater rock, deposit her eggs and perpetuate the species.

Though some anglers moisten a wet fly immediately after knotting it to their leader, it can be sound strategy to cast the fly dry and submerge it by giving the leader a pull or two while it is still upstream from the position of the trout. It will possess a delicate, silvery film of air which disappears after a trout takes it or after it becomes well soaked. You may speculate upon the mysterious powers of the fur-bodied flies by comparing them, under water, with any caddis fly you catch and submerge for research purposes. Trout who discover such a fly approaching them will often take it at any depth, so be prepared for action at any moment.

Figure 27. Stone fly

STONE FLY

Three centuries ago Charles Cotton wrote in *The Compleat Angler* of the trout's greed for stone flies. 'Matadores for trout and grayling,' he called them, 'remarkable, both for their size . . . and for the execution they do.' Big and durable enough for impaling on a hook, the natural fly is often dapped, floated or drifted by bait fishermen with impressive results. Particularly in the Midlands and the North Country, the stone fly has been and will always be a charmer of trout and fly fishermen.

The mated flies crawl about, fly over or simply fall into the water, sometimes in pairs. The eggs are deposited on the water by the flying or floating female, and the cycle begins again when the eggs stick somewhere on the stream bed near where they are dropped.

Quite properly, the stone fly is usually fished as a dry fly. A heavy, thick-bodied fly, it rests low in the water right in the surface film. During the day, however, trout cannot be coaxed to the surface as readily as one might prefer, and at such times a sunken stone fly may succeed, for it is one of the choicest morsels on any river for trout of all sizes.

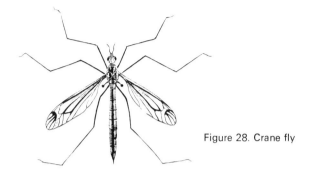

Figure 28. Crane fly

MIDGE, MOSQUITO, GNAT, CRANE FLY

An order of insects often ignored by fly fishermen due to the smallness of the larva and pupa, the Diptera are nonetheless essential for deceiving trout under those conditions where the fish are feeding selectively, as they frequently do in the still water of lakes and ponds where the Diptera abound.

The crane fly is a large-scale version of the mosquito. Some are aquatic, some spend just the larval stage in the water and pupate on land. The adult female dips to the water to deposit her eggs.

Figure 29. Dragonfly

61

DAMSEL FLY, DRAGONFLY

Similar in design, with protruding, segmented tube-like bodies and iridescent, transparent wings, these two flies also have similar life cycles. The smaller damsel fly is not as fast a flyer nor as powerful as the dragonfly, but both are superb flyers adept at catching and killing lesser insects in mid-air.

Figure 30. Alder fly

ALDER FLY

This is probably one of the best known of the angler's flies, mainly because it is very common, and is to be found near all types of water, mostly in the early part of the season around May and June. It is very similar in appearance to some dark medium-size sedges (caddis), having the same roof-shaped wings when at rest.

Figure 31. Alder larva

A characteristic of the fly is that the females lay their eggs on the underside of logs, rocks, bridges or plants, so that the larvae fall to the water when they hatch out. They then sink to the bottom where they live in the silt and mud. When they are ready to become winged insects they do not swim to the surface as do other types, but crawl ashore to bury themselves in the ground, forming cells in which they pupate. When the adult flies are ready to emerge from the pupa, they work their way up to the surface, where the final moult takes place and the fully winged flies appear. This fly is often fished wet as well as dry.

62

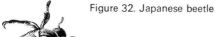
Figure 32. Japanese beetle

Figure 33. Wasp

LAND-BRED INSECTS

The various insects discussed here are all land-bred, and consequently their only interest to fly fishermen is their availability to trout through the air. The beetles, ants, bees and grasshoppers are particular favourites of the fly fishermen as dry flies, of course, for these insects often float momentarily when they are blown into or fall upon the water. Poor swimmers, they are soon sucked beneath the surface by the currents or the trout. There, if they survive, they kick their legs and struggle for a while in the manner of a drowning stone fly or even a swimming caddis.

Figure 34. Grasshopper

Like the big stone flies, the beetles and grasshoppers are large enough to be tossed into the currents for locating trout, a useful tactic on those days when the angler is

Figure 35. Ant

anxious for a big one. The type of rise will usually reveal the size of the fish. Once a big trout is located, the angler has gained valuable knowledge and may adjust his leader, his fly and his strategy to fit the situation.

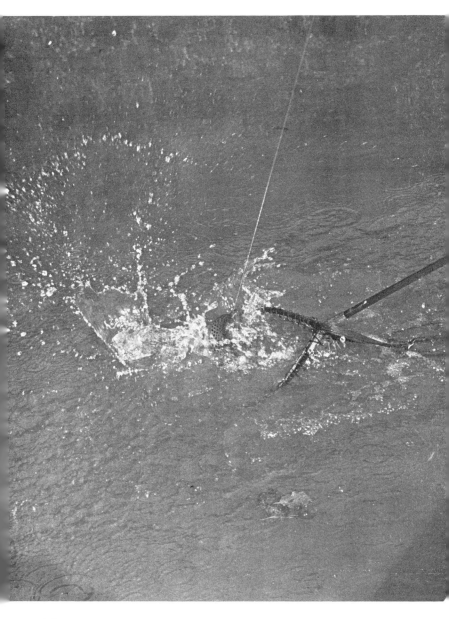

A fighting trout

65

A typical rough stream

9 Strategy on the Stream

Everyone who fishes for trout with an artificial fly will agree that the really great fascination of the sport lies in the challenging problems of stream strategy. The strategist allows not only for the habits and moods of the trout and the behaviour of its insect food, but also for the whole character of each stretch of stream; the speed of the currents, the depth of water, the variations in pools and riffles, the surface winds, the sunlight and shadow and an infinity of immobile stage props – trees, bushes, rocks and logs.

The real reward of the observant and skilful angler lies in his ability to plan an attack that penetrates the natural defences of the trout, tempts it to strike his lure and brings it through obstacles to the net. The angler who twitches minnow-like bucktails or streamers is counting for his sport on the capacity of such lures to excite the rapacity of the trout. The fisherman who uses larval-type, weighted nymphs, splashing them into the water so that they plummet to the bottom, is counting on the fundamental hunger of the fish. The dry-fly angler seeks to deceive rising trout at the surface. The angler who aspires to the pleasures of nymph and wet-fly fishing carries out his intrigue against the trout with feathers fragile and exuberant enough to create the illusion of an insect alive in the water.

The dry fly's bushy, stiff hackles enable it to ride on the surface film. The wet fly's sparser, softer hackle fibres quiver and kick beneath the surface. As the dry fly can be bounced or twitched about the surface to tantalise trout, so the nymph and wet fly can be manoeuvred in the water to act as if alive.

On the following pages you will learn the finer points of stream strategy, tactic by tactic, as they apply to typical stream conditions. First, however, you should know something of the basic ecological features of the water as all experienced anglers understand them.

The currents of a stream are food lanes and trout are attracted to them by hunger. Figure 36 shows a cutaway section of a stretch of typical trout water. Other factors, such as the urge to protect themselves, may divert the trout but, in the main, fish are found where the food is.

As a rule, the main current carries the bulk of the food supply during the day, whether insects are hatching or not. Stray insects such as beetles, bees and ants that are blown into or drop to any part of the surface of the stream, are usually drawn into the main current.

Secondary currents of lesser velocity at the sides of the main current are the areas generally preferred by trout, since the fish can hold its position in such areas with less effort. Hovering in the secondary current, the trout can swerve into the main current for insects going by or move into quieter water where, if it is deep, the trout may forage for nymphs or struggling insects. During the

Figure 36. The currents of a stream

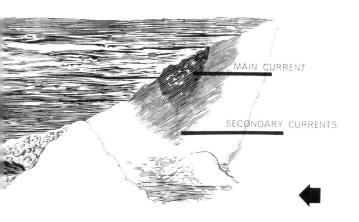

day trout usually shun the shallows, which offer little concealment from predators.

In fishing uncomplicated water, cast first into the relatively quiet water short of the main current. Such an area is not as likely to hold trout as the lane of secondary velocity farther out, where the broken surface water offers better concealment from their enemies, and where the trout can wait for food sweeping by in the main current. But the quiet water sometimes does yield trout; in any case, if the fly is cast there first, then advanced, cast by cast, into more promising areas the trout, wherever it is, will see the fly before it sees either the leader or the more disturbing ripples and shadows made by the line.

When the angler advances his fly beyond the main current, as in Figure 36, he runs into a common, recurring problem: drag. Any fast current that drags on line or leader causes the fly to move unnaturally fast. Sometimes the simple expedient of holding the rod high so that the line enters the water beyond the main current solves the problem.

Often, however, when fishing beyond the main current, you must resort to a manoeuvre known as 'mending' your cast. To mend your cast, you first release a little slack line through the guides. Then, by simply flicking your wrist, you impart a circling motion to the tip of your rod, which will throw a loop of the slack line upstream. With this extra slack on the water, your fly for a little time is undisturbed and unaffected by drag.

If you are fishing a remote area, or any stream recently stocked with small fish, you can at times fish carelessly, unmindful of drag, and still take trout. From such carefree luck you might come to assume that drag is not a deterrent to catching trout. Indeed almost any size or pattern of fly pulled across the water or beneath it may sometimes attract unsophisticated trout, since they are often so abundant and food consequently so scarce that they will fight for your fly. Even among the wildest trout, however, you may observe that it is the smaller fish that are most easily deceived.

As fish mature – especially those in our more heavily fished waters – they become increasingly sensitive to drag and other unnatural actions of a fraudulent fly that signal your presence. Whatever the nature of the trout stock, you should always try to minimise drag; only use heavy leaders when necessary; always wade cautiously and avoid disturbances caused by wading, casting un-natural shadows on the water or making sudden move-ments within view of fish. Though these seem to be inconsequential matters, such violations can scare the more desirable trout. Violation of the streamside rules will bring a penalty to the angler, as surely as do rules violations to participants in other sports.

If streams were structured as simply as the one illus-trated in Figure 36, there would be little more you would need to know than the behaviour of trout, their food and the effects of currents. But few streams are as simple, and on the following pages the finer points of strategy are covered as they apply to the true, complicated character of typical streams.

A POOL'S HIDDEN HAZARDS

The stream illustrated in Figure 37 presents a fairly common but always intriguing problem of strategy. The moment you approach the bank of the pool shown in the foreground, you watch for trout feeding at the surface. If there is no surface activity, you can still pre-sume trout are feeding beneath the surface, as they do most of the time on all streams. On a pool which looks as promising as this one, a well-presented fly could produce a fish almost anywhere. And here, as on many pools of medium size, you might cast from any of several positions. Your choice of position – indeed, your whole plan of attack – depends on what your ambitions are. Will you settle for any fish, or do you want a large one, perhaps the largest in the pool?

If you want a large trout, the place to present your fly is near the half submerged rock on the far side of the

Figure 37. Pool Strategy

main current. On the downstream side of this rock, decently concealed from predators by the broken water eddying around it, a trout can hover with ease on the edge of the food-laden current. Logic would indicate that the trout by the rock is a good one. The best trout are usually found in the best places.

You can cast to the rock from the bank in the fore-ground – but should you? If you reconnoitre along the bank, you will notice sunken logs crisscrossed out in the stream. Below these, the current smashes into driftwood

piled against the bank and sweeps into the riffle below. A large trout played from the near bank could create crisis after crisis amidst these obstacles and be lost at the logs, the driftwood or in the fast water below.

If you can get to it, the small island just beyond the rock is a far better casting position. On the island you would not be casting across the main current. There would be no drag, and the shorter cast from this spot would enable you to present the fly more temptingly. Moreover, once you hooked a fish from the island, the pull of your rod would be *away* from the logs. The island, therefore, is your choice.

The fast riffle between the bank and the island is deep and impassable, but farther downstream you have access across broad shallows. As you wade to the island, you will note that both the shallows and the deep riffle seem free of obstacles – a clear path for both the trout and you to the big water below, where a large fish can be played, exhausted and netted.

Once on the island, standing well back, you cast upstream so that your fly sinks before it drifts back to the rock. You guide the fly past the side of the rock away from you, in the current that brings food to the trout. As the fly passes the rock, you raise your rod tip with a slow, gradual motion that causes the fly to rise naturally towards the surface. You pivot your body, following through with the lifting motion, until the fly reaches the surface 1·8 or 2·4 m past the rock. The trout may strike just below the rock or he may follow the fly downstream to inspect it.

Your lifting motion imparts a lifelike movement to the hackle fibres and forces a decision from the trout, since the fly is escaping in a way that the trout readily recognises as the behaviour of many hatching insects.

You may see a swirl or flash of colour near your fly at any time, but more often the fish will rush as the fly approaches the surface. If there is no strike, let the fly float along a couple of metres more, imitating another characteristic of many insects.

When the trout strikes, set the hook – but not with a sharp jerk. A lift of the wrist will do it – at the instant you see the flash of colour or swirl near the surface. If the fish you hook at the rock is big, it will be several minutes before you can attempt to net him safely. Since he is familiar with all the aspects of the pool, you can expect him to surge towards the logs, a haven where he has gained freedom often, probably, when less circumspect anglers hooked him from the wrong bank. If he heads for the logs, exert pressure on the rod and try to steer him away. Should he get under them, he may sulk there only

74

A typical loch scene

Stalking the trout

briefly and, hopefully, come out the way he went in. Your pressure should be firm but not excessive. Success with a big trout often depends on such small matters.

But even if he does not get into the driftwood, the trout with his full strength can cause you trouble at any time by surfacing and rolling. During a surface roll, relax your rod pressure to avoid breaking the leader or tearing the hook out. If he turns towards the driftwood area of deep, fast water, encourage him to leave the pool by steering him firmly into the avenue of fast water leading downstream. Follow him down, rod held high to keep as much line as possible out of the water as he strips it and part of the backing from the reel. You still have to play him out, recover lost line and bring him to net, but at this point, with nothing save open, easy-moving water between you and the fish, the strategic battle is won.

In this situation, you have avoided the old bugbear, drag, presented your fly more temptingly to the trout and minimised the hazards of the stream. The big trout of the pool is your reward for planning the whole campaign well.

TACTICS FOR QUIET WATER

As free of obstacles as a swimming pool, the long, deep flat in Figure 38 presents few problems once a trout is hooked, but it is a good test of your tactical skills. Bright sunlight in this clear water exposes trout to their enemies so well that, unless a stiff breeze ruffles the surface, desirable fish are seldom active during the day. Early in the morning or late afternoon, when dim light prevails, such water will yield trout. Small fish may venture up from the bottom or out from the banks for a fly at any time of day, but the larger trout seek cover under the bushes along the left bank or hide in the shadows or beneath the grass covered, undercut bank on the right.

You may often hook trout in such water regardless of breeze or time of day with a technique first used by the ancient Greeks called dapping. In dapping on this stream,

Figure 38. Flat water strategy

your target is the trout concealed near the bank. On a
bank where the trout is virtually underfoot, naturally
you must step lightly to avoid vibrations. You should
stand as far back as possible to keep your shadow from
the water. Then, using a fly that imitates such favourite
trout food as the black ant, with a short line or only the
leader hanging from the rod tip, you touch your fly
gently to the grass at the bank edge and allow it to fall

naturally from the grass to the water. Dapping is delicate, often blind fishing: the slightest movement of the leader is significant. Large trout often sip in the fly silently and splash only after they feel the hook.

Playing a fish here, where there are no logs, rocks or fast water, is largely a matter of keeping the fish away from roots and out of the pockets under the bank. After a fish is hooked, you improve your chances of netting the

Safely netted!

fish by stepping into the shallows near the bank. Although advanced, more sophisticated anglers may look down on dapping as 'cheating', the fisherman who enjoys hooking, playing and netting trout will not ignore this method as a way of taking his fish.

When no insects are visible but you see fish rising under the bushes along the left bank, it is quite possible that they are feeding on tiny midges. Tie on a small Black Gnat and use a point no larger than 4x. With a side-arm cast, put your fly in under the bushes upstream from the spot where you have seen a fish rise. As your fly nears the fish, be ready to lift your rod tip on the slightest provocation. Your fly will be on or just beneath the surface, and any slight sign near your fly should be interpreted as a striking fish.

On an overcast day, good-sized fish may feed on flies hatching or drifting at various depths anywhere in this stretch of stream. Fishing a sunken fly representing the insects you see in the air is a reasonable tactic at such times. A long, fine leader and a light line are important: finesse and delicacy in presenting your fly are a vital part of your strategy. On smooth, clear water a slight ripple is very noticeable, and a heavy line or leader will cast stark shadows on the bottom.

TRICKS IN MIXED WATER

In water like that shown in Figure 39, you may fish a wet fly first at the surface, a tactic that might bring a trout in a splashing surface rise such as dry-fly fisher-men cherish. The fast main current sweeps past the outer side of the half-submerged boulder in the stream. In-shore from this boulder is inviting, productive water – a collecting area of insects flying against, or blown against, the steep bank edging the stream. Logically, fish often lie in this relatively quiet backwater, waiting for such easy pickings.

Though most anglers believe wet flies should be tied on heavy hooks, many patterns may be tied on light

CURRENT

wire hooks so that they drop lightly to the surface, float for a few moments and respond more realistically to the changing forces of the water. Upwinged flies, sedge flies, stone flies and ants touch the water lightly and often float momentarily, until pulled down in a swirl of water. They move wherever the current may take them – into an eddy or a backwater, down behind a boulder and up again. Many insects, caught temporarily in the current, are submerged only to rise to the surface again, float

Figure 39. Mixed water strategy

along low in the water and crawl back to safety on a tree limb or rock.

In fishing a collecting area where insects drop, it is a good idea to use a fly tied on a light wire hook, and barely touch it to the water on your first cast or two. On the piece of water in Figure 39, you would try the very edge of the stream, along the base of the bank. Touch the fly briefly and withdraw it. In this way you may tease and excite trout. Then, after false-casting once or twice to dry the

83

Figure 40. Fishing a big pool

CURRENT

fly, allow it to float on the surface film for a few metres downstream over any eager trout that might be lying there.

The current on both sides of the half-submerged boulder (see Figure 39 again) is strong, and any trout there is probably holding close to the boulder. Here you can make the rock itself work for you. A fly cast upstream sweeps by too fast to have much effect. Since there may be trout feeding out in the fast water, one approach is to cast your fly upstream, and as it drifts down, guide it towards the area below the boulder. Here, where there is less direct pull of the current, the churning water of the eddy will activate the hackles of a sunken fly. Another approach is to cast your fly into the pocket of water below the boulder so that your leader falls across the rock. In this position the fly may float and move free of drag. This tactic is often useful with dry as well as wet flies.

In fast water, a heavy wire hook is often good for sinking the fly to greater depths, where trout often feed. Bear this in mind the next time you visit a tackle shop. For if you equip yourself with hooks of varying weights, you will have both a light touch on the surface and also an effective lure in the depths.

FISHING A BIG POOL

A trout stream may cascade through ravines and run fast and wide in shallows, but here or there, sooner or later, almost all streams slow down and for a moment lose their force in a large, deep pool. In these pools the normal food lanes all but disappear. The water is calm and looks easy to fish; but such pools hold challenges, testing the angler's casting skill and his knowledge both of fish behaviour and of insect behaviour above and below the surface.

Desirable trout often rest during the day in the deepest water, difficult to reach with the small flies which some anglers prefer for this type of fishing. In such water the angler must fish far and fine, not only lengthening his casts to reach the more distant points but also using extra-long leaders, tapered to 4x, 5x or even 6x and tied to nymph-like flies of the smallest sizes. To the casual fishermen these minute particles of feather and fur may appear laughable, but as an angler matures on the streams he comes to appreciate their value in winning trout.

At dawn and dusk, trout stream insects often become quite active. Hatching nymphs swim upwards through the water, take wing, fly about to mate, then drop to the surface where the females deposit their eggs. During a hatch at dusk, particularly, the surface of a pool is broken by the swirls of feeding fish. The novice assumes the trout are feeding on floating flies. Quite often he is right; this can be the dry-fly fisherman's finest hour.

Figure 41. Caddis pupa (enlarged)

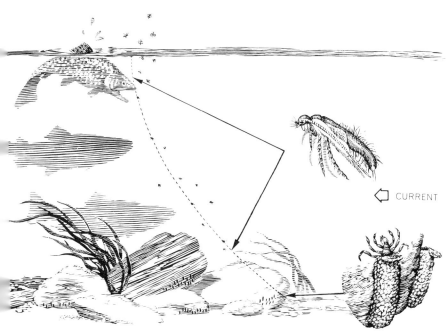

CURRENT

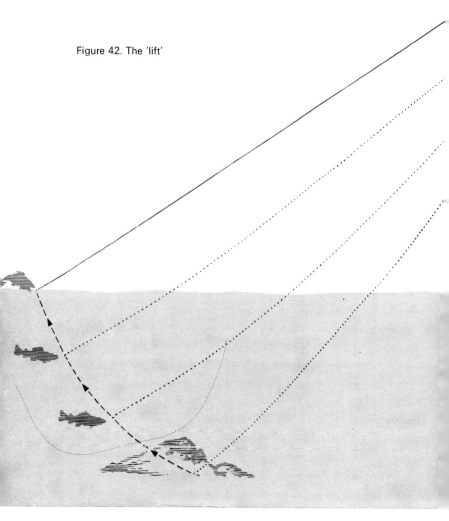

Figure 42. The 'lift'

Equally as often, however, the angler may be mystified and frustrated; he sees trout swirling everywhere, yet his dry fly floats along untouched. Why? In this whirl of activity, when trout seem to be feeding on floating insects, they are often feasting on swimming nymphs just beneath the surface, 2 or 3 cm below the domain of the dry-fly fishermen. There in the dim light of dusk the trout are safe from all their enemies except the angler skilled in the use of the lifelike nymph.

In fact, here virtually at the surface, at the crucial moment of the insect's metamorphosis into the mature fly, the essential drama between insect and trout takes place with greatest intensity. The heart of this drama is the sudden exposure to the trout's view of a hatching insect struggling upwards naturally and about to escape.

Many species of insects emerge from cases or from hiding places among stones and swim upwards through the current in a curving path towards the surface. Trout feed on ascending pupae or other insect nymphs in the depths far more often than casual anglers realise: the angler notices it only when a trout swirls and splashes to take an insect close to the surface.

This phenomenon of escaping, free-swimming insects, like the caddis pupa shown enlarged in Figure 41, is so exciting to trout that an imitation of the action can be used not only during a hatch in a pool, but almost any time of day, wherever an angler can manoeuvre a sunken fly naturally. This technique – called the 'lift' – is performed by moving line and fly in the water as shown in Figure 42 on pages 88–89.

The lift, used whever the speed of the current is not excessive, imitates the behaviour of a hatching nymph. To perform the lift, cast upstream and allow the fly to sink. Then, as the fly nears the position of the trout, raise arm and rod gradually to cause the fly to lift naturally through the currents. The trout may take it at once or he may hesitate and inspect the fly as he follows it downstream momentarily, making his decisive move just before the fly escapes at the surface. Stream strategy, finesse and a delicate control of the fly are the decisive factors when using the lift.

FISHING STILLWATER

Although the traditional southern chalk streams offer the supreme enjoyment of dry fly fishing, they have become largely privately owned and, in any event, very expensive. Of course the trout fishing (usually wet fly) in the wilder parts of Wales and Scotland is still either very cheap or free but is, by its nature, rather inaccessible. However, during the last few years, trout fishing has been brought within the reach of everyone's pocket by the mushroom growth of reservoirs and man-made lakes stocked with trout. A charge levelled against them is that they contain too many tame, stew-fed fish which are too easily caught, but a trout is a trout for all that. Basic techniques are the same as for many other trout waters but they must be adapted for the increase in boat fishing over bank and the need to fish below the surface much of the time, especially in hot weather when the fish may be 9 m or more down. There is a temptation though, to think that all the fish are at the bottom and in the middle and this must be resisted. Bank fishing with a moderate length of line should produce as many fish as long-distance record casting and is much less tiring. Keep to first principles as for other forms of trout fishing – find out what the trout are feeding on, try to imitate it and cast it accurately and quietly.

The anglers' reward

10 Useful Information

ASSOCIATIONS

Salmon & Trout Association
Fishmongers' Hall
London Bridge
London EC4R 9EL
Sec: B H Catchpole
The governing body of the sport which, amongst other services, organises fly fishing courses for young people aged 12–18.

BOOK LIST

Further reading from the A & C Black Fishing Library:

Instructional

Bank Fishing for Reservoir Trout by Jim Calver.
The Confident Fly-Fisher by Cunliffe R Pearce.
Fishing the Dry Fly by Dermot Wilson.
The Pursuit of Stillwater Trout by Brian Clarke.
Small River Fly Fishing by James Evans.

Reference

A Dictionary of Trout Flies by A Courtney Williams.

Magazine

Trout and Salmon(EMAP National Publications Ltd) monthly.